BE ASSURED, YOU'RE IN THE RIGHT HANDS

Michele Howe Clarke has touched people around the world with her inspirational books, speaking engagements, private consultations, workshops and online classes. Here are a handful of testimonials for her work.

"Survival behavior has certain qualities and characteristics. Michele's book shares the qualities learned from her experience about survival behavior. Read what she has learned about surviving and thriving." *Dr. Bernie Siegel, author of Faith, Hope & Healing and A Book of Miracles*

"Michele is the embodiment of courage, conviction and chutzpah! After overcoming impossible odds, she emerged to teach us all the lesson that life is worth fighting for in line with a destiny of our own choosing. Her talk was not only enlightening, it was the spark that restarted my internal conversation about how I can live with more passion and purpose." *Ellen Bloom, CAO and Corporate Secretary, Carnegie Corporation of New York*

"Michele shares her insightful wisdom and perspective in a totally absorbable way. We can all learn from her powerful story of tragedy to transformation – whether we are faced with a crisis in our lives, or even if we are just having a bad day. Michele has

made some incredible lemonade with the lemons life has handed her. I extend my gratitude to her for sharing her story and life tools. Michele provides tools to stay inspired no matter what you face."
 Erika Rauscher , Executive Director, THANC (Thyroid, Head and Neck Cancer) Foundation

"I enthusiastically recommend Michele to any person experiencing the effects of cancer. She will clearly show how one can thrive into the future. I only wish that I could mandate that all medical students hear her speak as it will give them critical patient perspectives that could only make them better, more empathetic, and more complete care-givers." Dr. Peter Costantino, Executive Director, New York Head & Neck Institute at Lenox Hill Hospital

"Michele Howe Clarke is a true inspiration! She has turned tragedy into triumph, and shares her hard-won knowledge with a passion that lights up the room and inspires those around her. Thanks to Michele's amazing attitude, we now know that we, too, can be 'thrivers', no matter what life throws our way. Bravo, Michele!" Valerie Hope Goldstein, Facilitator, Boston Chapter, Support for People with Oral and Head and Neck Cancer (SPOHNC)

"Michele is an inspiring speaker who delivered an impassioned and engaging presentation to our staff. We were all deeply touched and she gave us cause to celebrate, to always be grateful of life's circumstances. Let us remember to face forward, indeed." Nadine S. Schneider, Director, Speakers Bureau, The Jewish Federations of North America

"I had been diagnosed with metastatic breast cancer. Your talk and book came at just the right time!! I felt so empowered. I memorized the "intention" sentences and every day I use them when I meditate. I just visited you Web site — and fell in love with you and your beautiful, powerful caring and healing ways. I am looking forward to the future with hope, joy, and gratitude with deep appreciation to you and your work. Many thanks." **Janet Vohs, Boston MA**

ABOUT THE AUTHOR

An award winning author, Michele Howe Clarke is founder of Face Forward You. She is a successful business woman with a B.A. in Psychology from Boston University, and M.B.A. from Howard University. She is a seasoned real estate investor, successful turnaround expert, QSCA certified life coach, and TEDx speaker.

Michele is a thriving survivor of head and neck cancer, which altered her facial features. Her critically acclaimed best seller *Face Forward, Meeting Challenges Head on in Times of Trouble* (Morgan James Publishing, 2012), tells her story of recovery and transformation. As a result, her survivor to thriver methodology shared through her books, personal development programs, and speaking engagements, has inspired many to overcome their own obstacles and bounce back better.

Michele Howe Clarke motivates people to face forward and live the best NOW possible. She specializes in surviving and thriving by Engaging Thrive Drive. Her focus on success principles, is the foundation of her philosophy to you live your best life now. To learn more about Michele Howe Clarke and building positive resiliency go to https://faceforwardyou.com/.

Face Forward Thrive Guide

FACE FORWARD THRIVE GUIDE

Michele Howe Clarke

LUXE BEAT MEDIA

Published by Luxe Beat Media, Raleigh, North Carolina.

All rights reserved. Copyright © 2018 Michele Howe Clarke

Although the author and publisher have made every effort to ensure that the information in this book was correct at press time, the author and publisher do not assume and hereby disclaim any liability to any party for any loss, damage, or disruption caused by errors or omissions, whether such errors or omissions result from negligence, accident, or any other cause.

e-Book
ISBN-10: 1-941065-09-0
ISBN-13: 978-1-941065-09-9

Print
ISBN-10: 1-941065-08-2
ISBN-13: 978-1-941065-08-2

Library of Congress Number available upon request.

No part of this book may be reproduced or transmitted in any form or by any means, electronic or mechanical, including photocopying, recording, or by any information storage and retrieval system, permitted by law. The only exception is by a reviewer, who may quote short excerpts in a review. For permission to copy, go to www.faceforwardyou.com.

DEDICATION

For Dwayne, Sage and Malachi – my three hearts that give my life rhythm.

And for my mom, Esme, who helps me find my voice.

Contents

This is where you start 1
Foreword by a phoenix rising 6

Part I: The lay of the land

Get your bearings 9

One is not an average 12

You are one powerful energetic being 14

Be present 16

Using your internal compass to navigate 18

Say 'yes' when you mean 'yes' 20

Own your authentic 'no' 22

The real deal of your story 24

Bye bye habit's ponsy 26

Build up belief in Y.O.U. 28

Part II: It's all about Y.O.U.

The tenets of Y.O.U. 31

It's time to thrive 34

The power of Y.O.U. 36

Rules of the road 38

World of contrast 40

Receive/believe 42

Faith, the door to enthusiasm 44

Step into a bright future 46

Help the subconscious help Y.O.U. 48

Imagination is your workshop 50

What you are thinking is making you feel 52

Feel your way forward 54

Harness power 56

Constructing the reality of Y.O.U. 58

Be what you seek 60

Come home any time 62

Reinforce Y.O.U. 64

Part III: Engaging Thrive Drive

Your heart leads you to Reach 67

Master fear 68

Apply your power 70

Necessity, the mother of skill 72

Imagination, a master's workshop 74

When all else fails, laugh 76

Leading questions to create your life your way 78

Leading questions work for Y.O.U. 80

Get enthused 82

Positive constructive thoughts 84

Y.O.U. and M.E. 86

Deliberately choose 88

The greatest discovery of all 90

Confidently step out 92

Master fortune 94

Fear's illusion 96

AARRCC into Y.O.U. 98

Cause in effect 100

It's a mastery thing – we will practice for a lifetime 102

Part IV: Flip on the Power Switch

Plant a seed for tomorrow wisely 105

Happily fill free time 106

Keep an open mind 108

A plan to direct your efforts 110

Have fun, play with choice 112

Purposeful passion glittering on your horizon 114

Weight the scales of your day more positively 116

Feel the sun 118

Take a load off 120

You've got the power 122

Use powerful of language 124

Dream it up 126

Breathe life 128

Breath works for Y.O.U. 130

Part V: Energy life map

Working energy 133

The seven energy centers 136

Root Center 140

Navel Center 142

Solar Plexus Center 144

Heart Center 146

Throat Center 148

Brow Center 150

Crown Center 152

Part VI: Color Magic

Color your life with magic 155

Red Magic 158

Orange Magic 160

Yellow Magic 162

Green Magic 164

Blue Magic 166

Indigo Magic 168

Violet Magic 170

Personal invitation from Michele (and secret pass) 172

Face Forward: Meeting Challenges Head On in Times of Trouble (Morgan James Publishing 2012)
175

THIS IS WHERE YOU START

I think therefore I am. – Rene Descartes

Welcome to Face Forward Thrive Guide, you are where you need to be. It's all about Y.O.U. (Your Own Uniqueness), your divine design, the excellence only Y.O.U. can shine in this life.

First I want to acknowledge you for showing up in your life and taking action on your own behalf. Good on you! 80% of success is showing up. Please take a moment and congratulate yourself for being an intentional creator.

Change is inevitable and you know it. You have the power to flip the script, and you are about to have a blueprint of what to do next. Here you will learn how to take back your control and stop the needless suffering. The key here is that you recognize that you have power to change. Your life is in your control; you are in charge. You will build trust in yourself, believe you can.

There are only two ways to live your life. One is as though nothing is a miracle. The other is as if everything is. -Albert Einstein

Listen, I walk this thriving journey with you, daily I must master suffering through shifting my perceptive mindfully. Aggressive facial cancer shattered my picture perfect life, a new mom I was broken like Humpty Dumpty. First, I had to overcome serious mortal odds to survive then I had to learn how to live gracefully with a paralyzed face. From the rubble of a broken life I had to learn to thrive through and beyond the dire statistics, thrive past the odds of what seemed possible.

An inherent drive propels me to be the cause of my intended effect. Innovating out of troubles has become my expertise. Over 10,000 hours of study, use and teaching helped me to flourish disfigured and created the means to engage innate thrive resources.

It's all about Y.O.U., aligning with Your Own Uniqueness, the excellence only you can share. You came programmed like an acorn to be a great oak. My job is reminding you that it's Time to Thrive!

I had to sacrifice my "normal face" for a chance at a new extraordinary life. Through this transformational experience with disfiguring head and neck cancer, I learned to say "Yes?" and "Next!". I had an abrupt and painful conclusion followed by a wondrous beginning.

I am transformed like a phoenix rising from the ashes. I am reborn with purpose and vitality. My transformational journey is detailed in my award winning book _Face Forward: Meeting Challenges Head On in Times of Trouble_ (2012).

If you permit me, I will share with you a path to your power, a door to cultivating a positive approach to become a flexible and adaptable navigator. My question to you is: – are you ready to try something new with a positive spirit? ... Yes?... YES!

Great! Now let's set our intention so may we access innate resources to manifest purposefully: We intend this information support and expand our possibilities to live our highest and best life. So be it, so it is.

This amazing technology is all about Y.O.U. resiliently cultivating a positive approach to anything life throws at you. You will learn to thrive along your natural lines of growth to be where you want to be. Along the way, as you stay in the flow of your divine design, you will begin to feel better and better.

You can reach for relief and end the needless suffering. The key here is that you recognize that you can say YES to Y.O.U. You will build trust in Y.O.U. and enthusiastic faith will bloom as the good you have caused keeps appearing at your door. All you need do is begin.

Do or do not, there is no try. – Yoda

THE THRIVE GUIDE IS AS EASY AS ABC

This is a take you by the hand kind of a book. Let go of your fear, we are building faith here. Faith is certainty of a positive outcome built on nothing but your agreement. This journey was created with the intention of unlocking the excellence of Y.O.U. We want the light of Y.O.U. to come pouring into your life.

The content unfolds in a step by step process that leads to

your natural lines of growth. You will feel the good flow as you align and harmonize with Y.O.U.

The practice is simple. You read the daily practice and allow the information to take root day by day. The quote helps fill your head with power.

The journey is winding and you meet lessons again and again on this spiral learning staircase. Transformation tends to cause you to meet yourself on the road and face old negative behavior resurfacing as you expand past your normal boundaries.

Engaging Thrive Drive is a process so give it a moment to catch root, gain strength and grow in your life. Along the journey you will feel yourself shining up, like polishing a tarnished gem. The good will flow as you flip on the switch of your excellence.

Let's get you thriving sooner faster quicker with your complimentary Life Reset Challenge. Grab your gift at /https://faceforwardyou.com/free-5-day-life-reset/

FOREWORD BY A PHOENIX RISING

What can I say about Michele Howe Clarke?

Here's a woman whose perfect life was shattered the day she received a dreaded diagnosis – the day an aggressive facial cancer destroyed her dreams

Who she was, everything she did, her future plans – and what she looked like – all changed in a moment.

A successful investment banker and a new mom, Michele was thrown into a place none of us would want to be. Yet, this woman is cut of a different cloth. She is, to use her phrase, an "adversity navigator" with an inherent drive and a will to thrive that is, quite frankly, astonishing to witness.

After the success of her award-winning, bestselling first book *Face Forward: Meeting Challenges Head on in Times of Trouble*, Michele knew she was only getting started with her message for the world.

You see, even disfigured, her life completely altered, Michele continued to flourish. She learned to innovate through troubles, time and time again, and this became her passion – and her expertise.

As we all know, not every surprise in life is a pleasant

or easy one. And, understandably, most people feel lost, broken or to blame during difficult times.

Experience taught Michele that with every challenge there is a hidden gem, a portal of strength that births us into the next brilliant version of ourselves.

All you need are the right tools to find your brilliance. The very tools Michele discovered during her transformational journey, which taught her how to face forward, survive and ultimately thrive.

Now in the *Thrive Guide*, Michele shares how you too can reach for relief and end needless suffering. The key is to discover Y.O.U. or "Your Own Uniqueness". Like the acorn that comes programmed to become a great Oak tree, Y.O.U. is the seed of greatness you came into this world with, already programmed, it's the brilliance only you can share.

In working with the *Thrive Guide*, you will build trust in Y.O.U. With Michele as your guide, no matter what you are facing, no matter how hard things appear, no matter what life throws at you, you will find that you too can THRIVE.

Kristen Moeller, MS, bestselling author of *Waiting for Jack* and *What Are You Waiting For?*, Literary Agent, Waterside Productions, Executive Publisher, Persona Publishing

PART I: THE LAY OF THE LAND

GET YOUR BEARINGS

Your pain is the breaking of the shell that encloses your understanding. – Kahil Gibran

Do you find yourself asking – WHY ME?

Sometimes it can feel like the walls of your life fall down leaving you standing alone as you meet yourself on the road. You take a hard look out at what was and now the what is. You can see the past is gone and but the future looks so hazy. There is no more surety; instead you may only find uncertainty, doubt and fear.

When you are not where you want to be, you may look around comparing and questioning: WHY ME? Why this? Why now?

But the true question is: Does everything you have taken for granted in your life come crashing to clarity? Does hope beat in your chest when you think of the future?

I want you to flip your Why? to How? How can I evolve gracefully through this?

Let's quickly get to the root of your life's challenges by

first going to the cause instead of looking at the effects. Answer this critical question... Do you believe the universe is friendly or unfriendly? Decide your course. Is life for you or against you?

Know now, it is your choice. Decide and make this vital choice for your highest and best. See the glass as 1/2 full. This is Y.O.U. building the muscle of active faith.

ONE IS NOT AN AVERAGE

We live in a wonderful world that is full of beauty, charm, and adventure. There is no end to the adventures that we can have if only we seek them with our eyes open. – Jawaharial Nehru

You are not a statistic. No really, listen up, you are one person so it's all or nothing. There are no averages for Y.O.U., there is only a 100% chance or a 0% chance.

Let this knowledge help you get your head in the game. Begin to move in a new direction and rely on Y.O.U. instead of "what they say". Become the captain of your life. You are here reading this. You are in motion, taking positive action on your own behalf. GOOD ON YOU. Congratulate yourself. No really take a second and please praise Y.O.U.

View yourself with deep appreciation and reverence. Treat yourself as you would a small child with love and care. Self cherishing is a powerful evolutionary progression of an empowered human being.

YOU ARE ONE POWERFUL ENERGETIC BEING

If we all did the things we are capable of doing we would literally astound ourselves. – Thomas Edison

Can you imagine yourself looking at a star and saying that it is worthless just out there twinkling?

But you have no problem taking yourself down a notch or down 100 notches for that matter. We women are our own harshest critics, always finding fault in ourselves. It is easy for us to condemn ourselves to a life of suffering, believing we are never good enough and not worth it.

OY VEY! the things we allow to run around in our heads. We war against our own selves. We spend our spare time worrying about the future and the past when really we have nothing but the present. It is our gift.

Many of us struggle with the idea that we are worthy. We need to step into the space of inherent value and own that we are valuable, period. We are alive and therefore valuable. We do not have to earn this right, our birth certified it.

It is from this place of value that I ask you to approach all things. Stand in your significance. You are here, a precious resource. Nurture your value as if it were a baby. Hold it with love and look upon it with the faith you would an infant, full of infinite possibilities.

It is time to be sick to death of that nagging voice always finding fault. Now I ask you to believe in Y.O.U., in Your Own Uniqueness, in your divine design. Trust the Navigator of Y.O.U. to lead you along your natural lines of growth.

You are alive therefore you are precious. Honor yourself, refocus, become present and mindful that Y.O.U. are the cause of your effects.

BE PRESENT

Be here now. – Ram Dass

The past is just a memory and the future is a dream. Now is a present because it is the cause both effects. Accept the fact that you are living in this moment and no other moment exists.

Allow life to flow, do not fight the current. You can use your power of choice by simply noticing that you have a choice. You have the option to stay in process.

Oversee your perception and notice all the possibilities available in this moment. The path is the goal, it is in the getting there that the 'be' of your cause occurs. Be present and meet yourself with compassion, observe without judgment.

If you listen to your heart you will discover what really gives meaning and purpose to your life. Begin to consistently follow heart inspiration and find love as the cause your life effects. Get fully involved in what inspires you, listen to and trust your heart to activate your internal compass.

USING YOUR INTERNAL COMPASS TO NAVIGATE

The future belongs to those who believe in the beauty of their dreams. – Eleanor Roosevelt

Tuning up your thrive drive releases your internal compass. Your internal compass navigates to your personal horizon and releases your infinite potential.

Your internal compass is based on foundational triads of harmony and balance. Learning to follow the signs and signals of your internal compass leads you to where you want to be.

Let's meet the Triads that once balanced transforms life:

<u>Perception</u> > <u>Preference</u> > <u>Power</u> unlocks your story and your ability to flip the switch of your power.

<u>Heart</u> > <u>Brain</u> > <u>Guts</u> are your true intuition and understanding the impetuses of these will help you gain in clarity.

<u>Be</u> > <u>Do</u> > <u>Have</u> come from that state of being and you will have.

<u>Mind > Body > Spirit</u> all that we do must be accordance with these three.

<u>Thoughts > Words > Actions</u> when aligned we mean what we say, say what we mean and do what we say.

<u>Live > Love > Laugh</u> give our life vibrancy, where would we be without these?

<u>Serenity > Courage > Wisdom</u> to have the serenity to accept the things we cannot change, the courage to change the things we can, and the wisdom to know the difference.

<u>Belief > Enthusiasm > Faith</u> as you believe your enthusiasm of a bright future grows and you receive what you have caused your faith will then grow in accordance.

Always feel supported by the foundational triads of your internal compass. Each triad has three legs on which it stands; each leg helps support the other. Each triad can stand alone in times of need and support you.

Learning to masterfully align these supports in equilibrium frees your intuition and insight. By attaining balance in each triad you step into your flow of life and are directed in each step of your life-journey.

SAY 'YES' WHEN YOU MEAN 'YES'

Throw off the bowlines. Sail away from the safe harbor. Catch the trade winds in your sails. Explore. Dream. – Mark Twain

So many of us were programmed early on, to say "Yes", to everyone and everything, even when we truly want to answer "No". No. See, it's a complete sentence. There is no need to explain. If you do, it generally goes like this: "No, because ... (a lie)."

We tie ourselves up and down with obligations to other people, and we feel guilty if we let them down by saying "no" to their request. But, what of your time, the obligation you owe yourself?

It is of critical importance that you begin to say 'yes' when you mean 'yes' and 'no' when you mean 'no'. Instead of saying 'yes' when you really mean 'no'. It's time to start saying 'yes' to Y.O.U.

Many of us have never learned to say no, so everything is yes. It is easy to give yourself away cheaply. Whoever needs you gets you at your best but when Y.O.U. needs you there's nothing left to give. We can easily lose our own importance along the way.

Sometime soon just take a break from the tradition of obligation and give yourself the time to be alone to focus on you. Allow yourself space to shut down, to just stop thinking and planning. By taking yourself away from restricting ties you will float better out there in life's depths, buoying yourself up. Do what feels right for you. Lighten up on your insatiable obligation to please the world.

In crisis you may need to just hunker down and get ready instinctively to get through come hell or high water. In your life you may need to close chapters that are draining, perhaps even toxic. Do it! You do not need energy vampires sucking the life out of you. Go ahead and sever the ties that bind; these goodbyes are likely long overdue.

You can ask for space to deal, to find your way back to yourself and take ownership of the present. Sometimes you need time with no distractions, time to become better. You have spent enough time being what you thought everyone else wanted of you, now you can decide not to worry about what others think of you. It only matters what you think of Y.O.U. and how you focus your thoughts.

OWN YOUR AUTHENTIC 'NO'

The main thing is to keep the main thing the main thing. – Stephen Covey

From here on out decide, to speak up and ask for what you need. It's time to be the cause of your desired effect. Begin to answer only to Y.O.U.

Saying yes to Y.O.U. is a natural line of growth and leads you to an enhanced ability to set healthy boundaries. Free up wasted capacity to live better by letting the good flow.

In your every day, remember to value yourself. You are inherently valuable, you are worthy, like a tree... a river... a star. The key here is that you do not have to earn it.

Start making Y.O.U. a priority in your life. Own your authentic 'no'. Sprinkle it liberally in your life. Let the good flow to, from and of Y.O.U.

Now, let me ask you:
- What are the three main areas in which you are saying 'yes' when you mean 'no'?
- How are you going to change that and gain your value back?
- How will you celebrate Y.O.U.?

THE REAL DEAL OF YOUR STORY

A pessimist sees the difficulty in every opportunity; an optimist sees the opportunity in every difficulty. – Sir Winston Churchill

Tell me, did you ever wonder how your life ended up this way?

To be the cause of your desired effect it is vital to examine the real deal of your life story. Your perception is the filter through which you see the world, it is uniquely your own and like no other. You have created it. It's view frames the script that programs your life story.

Here are some keys to open the door to a shift in your perspective:

- Facts are cold and clinical, they have no emotion.
- Your emotional state is created by the story you tell around the facts of your life.
- An emotion is created when you focus on a thought for more than 15 seconds.
- What are you focusing on? You are always narrating your life. Ask if your narration is serving you.

- Begin to recognize the story you are weaving around the facts. Please observe yourself compassionately, meet yourself where you are without judgment.
- Know that you have done the best you could with what you had. Now, be aware that you have choices.

Everything you see and experience is influenced by your perception. You become what you concentrate on. If your perception is tinged with a steel gray of self doubt then your possibility is hampered.

If you are focused on what you do not want, you receive more of what you do not want. By becoming aware of your story you empower yourself to shift your perception to a more optimistic view. Begin to constructively master your inner dialogue.

As you delve into your perception, you will begin to wake up. Take back control by becoming present and aware of how you have been describing the facts of your life. Consciously ask if that story still serves you. See what truth remains in your life story.

BYE BYE HABIT'S PONSY

You become what you think about. – Earle Nightingale

We are all victims of habit. The habits of early childhood cling to us all, throughout our life. Habit is created by repeatedly directing one or more of your five senses in a given direction.

It is through this repetition, doing the same thing, thinking the same thoughts, repeating the same words over and over again, that a negative or positive habit is formed.

Once a habit is formed it can be likened to a groove in a record. Your mind like the needle easily fits in and seeks out that groove. It is from this familiarity that a false sense of safety develops.

Our subconscious is programmed to seek safety, so it is drawn, to repeat this habitual behavior over and over. Even if in reality, this habit has a negative impact.

When a habit is well formed, the mind has a tendency to attach itself to, and follow the course of that habit, closely seeking the ease and comfort of a well followed path. Your current operating program reflects the premise: better a known pain than an unknown...

Any habit may be discontinued by building a more desirable habit in its place. It is easiest to begin by habit-stacking, making small shifts in behavior that lead you in the right direction.

Nature hates a void leading us to fall back into what ever was there before. To create a new positive habit it is critical to fill the void left behind by breaking the bad habit.

Nothing can bring you peace or success but yourself. If you want more then be sure to demand more of Y.O.U. It is your choice whether you want to hold positive or negative habits. It can be your choice to navigate to Y.O.U. and feel the good flow.

BUILD UP BELIEF IN Y.O.U.

Most of the important things in the world have been accomplished by people who have kept on trying when there seemed to be no hope at all. – Dale Carnegie

It is good to believe inherently, that somewhere in your make–up, there is a subtle something which when aroused by the proper influence, will carry you to the heights of excellence. This is that subtle something is the excellence, you were born to share, it is uniquely of you and no one can realize it as well as you. This excellence is Y.O.U. ,Your Own Uniqueness, your perfect pattern, your divine design.

By believing in this excellence of Y.O.U. , you develop the habit of self confidence, which opens your mind to positive expectation thereby the muscle of faith is developed. Your biggest quest is to find the stimulus that inspires you to greater action and awakens the dormant forces lying within you.

The path to this stimulus becomes apparent as you focus on what makes you happy. The rule of habit is a pivotal point on which success or failure turns. Intend to acquire habits which lead you to move through life with an abundance of health, unfaltering faith, unflagging energy, unceasing optimism and unbounded confidence.

It's time to build a relationship with Y.O.U. Take action and change the harmful habits into constructive ones. Self confidence is a product of knowledge in action, a dynamic duo of learning and doing.

Unless you sit down and become acquainted with yourself, as you never have before, you will not know what strength, power and possibility lie within the discovery of your own self reliance.

Take the time to recognize what is helping and what is hindering you. Look at life like a scientist. You create a hypothesis and you test it. Be aware of the results you are causing.

Quantify those results; on a scale of 1 to 100; is this moving you forward or not? If not, then change the hypothesis and examine the cause and effect again.

Stay flexible and adaptable. Now Y.O.U. are navigating.

PART II: IT'S ALL ABOUT Y.O.U.

THE TENETS OF Y.O.U.

Do not wish to be anything but what you are, and try to be that perfectly. – St. Francis of De Sales

It's all about Y.O.U. Your Own Uniqueness, the excellence only you can shine in this life.

- Y.O.U. is a supremely intelligent highly responsive automated machine.
- Y.O.U. is the seed of excellence you came programmed with. Like a tiny acorn destined to be a great oak, you have a divine design, an amazing light of Your Own Uniqueness to shine.
- Unlocking the automation of Y.O.U. provides an express ticket home to comfort and safety anytime you need it.
- Attuning to Y.O.U. yields trust in events and meaning in all circumstances.
- Engaging the Thrive Drive provides you access to your Navigator.
- Your Navigator directs you to flow along your natural lines of growth with ease by steadfastly pointing toward your true north.

- As you keep your bright future in view and faith builds upon active faith, the muscle of your positive expectations grows in resiliency.

IT'S TIME TO THRIVE

Courage is not the absence of fear, but rather the judgement that something else is more important than fear. – Ambrose Redmoon

No one can do this for you but Y.O.U.. It's time to live authentically and create space for you to triumph. It's time to generate creativity and brilliantly transform the cause of your effect.

Its time to flip your script and reprogram your self confidence for success. It's time to navigate to a fulfilled life that you appreciate. Its time to be actively attractive, wield your power and direct the show.

Your emotional state is where you vibrate and the cause of your point of attraction. Like attracts like. You are sentencing yourself to despair or holding yourself to the heights of your possibility by the thoughts you think and thus the feelings you feel.

In course of time all that matters is what you are focusing on. Think about what you want and you will get it. Think about what you don't want and you will also get it.

You are mastering the simple, rinse and repeat practice of thinking about what you want more than what you do not want. This simple solution will weigh heavy in your success.

Now don't get me wrong, you must feel it to heal it. So I am not saying that you should only be positive all the time but to consistently shift your perspective toward what you can glean from experience.

We are going to work on reprogramming your operating system; scientifically reviewing causes do not work for you anymore and building new successful programs.

Know that it is okay to have some 'oh well' days; we are not trying to be perfect here, so please do not beat yourself up.

THE POWER OF Y.O.U.

Give me a lever long enough and a fulcrum on which to place it, and I shall move the world. – Archimedes

Most of our negative behaviors are just faulty programs running in our subconscious mind. If we were at the helm of our focus we would not consciously sabotage our progress. We can reprogram the subconscious mind by working with its primary tools of words and images.

The mind is made up of two parts, the conscious and the subconscious. The conscious mind houses our will power, our analytical skills, and our reasoning. The conscious mind is only about 15% of your mind. The remaining 85% is the subconscious mind that controls the mechanics of your body and is where imagination, emotion and all your beliefs are stored.

From birth to age eight you gather the beliefs that form your unique belief system. Your belief system is built experience upon experience. You create ideas in response to circumstances and habits of mind are born by simple repetition.

These habits of mind, if left alone, become the operating

programs that run your life. Onto every new circumstance the critical area of mind (your perception) projects these old beliefs again and again until they become the operating programs that you unconsciously live by.

If you are living defensively, you wake up every morning and go about life with beliefs that you happened to pick up along the way. Let's get strategic. You can now start by taking the offensive and asking: "Does this belief actually still work for me?" If it does not, you can shift it to something that serves Y.O.U.

Your subconscious beats your heart, breathes you, circulates your blood, houses your belief systems and your imagination. Begin now to build faith and trust in the process of the subconscious mind to positively lead you. Since you are the navigator, set the course and trust that that which beats your heart, will get you there, as sure as the sun rises.

RULES OF THE ROAD

It is never too late to be what you might have been. – George Elliot

Let's open the door to exponential performance, leverage this basic knowledge of the subconscious:
- it is always being programmed through 1 of 5 your senses.
- what goes in it, comes out of it.
- any question you ask it will be answered.
- it can be controlled by focusing the conscious mind.
- it holds a deep fear of the unknown which too can be soothed by the conscious mind.

Meditation is a powerful tool to use to create success in working with the subconscious. You can bring about great effects every time you enter an alpha state of mind.

The means of meditation is yours to define. The key is to use your imagination and get absorbed in your inner experience. Strengthening your imaging faculty is another key to thriving and best applied in an alpha state of awareness. Try out an imaging in your free gift pack at FaceForwardYou.com/freegiftpack.

Michele Howe Clarke

WORLD OF CONTRAST

The universe is full of magical things patiently waiting for our wits to grow sharper. – Eden Phillpotts

We operate in a world of contrast, in an ever expanding universe. We will always We always want to get from here to there. Once we get there we want to get somewhere else. Desire is born from this contrast. Breed in this same contrast is the discord of not being where you want to be.

This emotion of discord/dis-ease is indicating you are out of alignment with your natural lines of growth. By attuning to the indicators of your internal compass Y.O.U. deliberately create. Steps to bridge to the new desire from current limitations appear in your mind's eye. We came programmed with a preference system to help us navigate to our desires.

Emotions are your guide. Your preferences are Y.O.U., Your Own Uniqueness. Let Y.O.U. control your point of focus. Be the cause of the effect you seek. Proceed from your feeling state forward. You are being guided, your feelings are telling you how aligned you are with your natural lines of growth. You draw from your focus which becomes your feeling state.

RECEIVE/BELIEVE

What we see depends mainly on what we look for. – Sir John Lubbock

The subconscious mind accepts and acts upon all suggestions that reach it, whether they are constructive or destructive. It does not matter if the suggestion comes from Y.O.U. consciously, or if it comes as an unconscious effect of your environment.

Select a goal; then fix your conscious mind upon it with such intensity that it communicates with the subconscious mind and registers with it to develop the outline of the cause in effect. Meditate on the feeling of attaining your goal. Breathe in the celebration of your success.

With repeated practice you will see the great effects you caused in reality. You will develop faith and trust in the process. This confidence will increase the efficiency and effectiveness of your cause manifesting.

FAITH, THE DOOR TO ENTHUSIASM

Dreams are renewable no matter what our age. – Dale Turner

The way may not open suddenly, revealing clearly the path ahead, but take that first step toward your goal, and it will lead to the second. One step at a time, the course opens to Y.O.U.

When you become aware of an opportunity to take that first step, take it without hesitation. Do the same with all the subsequent steps essential for the attainment of your goal.

Continuous and intensified faith is a key ingredient for keeping any goal alive. Faith is a positive expectation. This positive expectation is based in nothing but belief.

When you continue to believe in attaining a positive result you build muscles of positive expectation. Positive expectation in an aspiration leads to enthusiasm. Enthusiasm adds excitement. The future looks brighter each time a positive effect you cause arrives in your life.

STEP INTO A BRIGHT FUTURE

Most people are about as happy as they make up their minds to be. – Abraham Lincoln

Remember to keep your mind in a state of enthusiastic expectancy for the attainment of your goal. One way of doing that, is to remind yourself as often as you can, that you are the of cause your effect. Breathe life into your aspiration. Act when inspired.

It is most important is that you believe you can get to where you want to go. Nothing can improve unless you place faith in Y.O.U. Start to build up belief systems that support Y.O.U.

Start to identify with the way you want to be. Feel forward, start with your thinking, your image of yourself, your words, your clothing, etc. and begin to express the future in the present.

We run programs initiated when we were young children, everything we have done in our life is recorded in our subconscious mind. We have a lot of programs about everything from food to love.

Some programs are useful, while the usefulness of others

has expired. It is time to get off autopilot. Dispel repeated points of frustration. Begin to tell another story. Flip you script to the polar opposite. Take a new view.

HELP THE SUBCONSCIOUS HELP Y.O.U.

To accomplish great things, we must not only act, but also dream; not only plan, but also believe. – Anatole France

The subconscious mind houses a deep fear of the unknown. It will prevent you from moving forward to a new goal if it is unknown it will think it is unsafe. If where Begin to soothe your subconscious and pave the way to your desired effect by connecting the word 'safe' with where you want to be.

When you feel a bad script/program running, sit down with piece of paper and ask: what am I feeling now? Try auto-writing, put you pen to paper and write for 45 seconds, this is like a window into what you are thinking. Let the feeling flow instead of pushing it back down.

For the most part, we think more about what we do not want rather than what we do want. Your mind is a very complex computer; basically what goes in comes out, nothing different. Your thoughts are the seeds you plant in your mind.

If you planted tomato seeds in your garden you would

not expect cabbages to grow. Yet, we do this with our lives all the time wishing and hoping for a better life but coming from a space of lack and fear. This will not cause the effect you seek.

If you look in the mirror and find something you do not like, you will find more disappointment appearing in your life. How on earth can you put one thing into your mind and then expect something different to come out? It does not work like that. If you continue to find fault with your life, how can you transform?

IMAGINATION IS YOUR WORKSHOP

Life is a great big canvas, and you should throw all the paint you can on it. – Danny Kaye

Take a look at all the man made inventions around you that make your life easier. Think about it. Stop for a moment and realize that at first each was just an idea in someone's head. First there was the idea then the object. Tap into the power of infinite possibilities to fuel your imagination, receive-/believe. A belief is only long held idea. It is time to make your beliefs causes of your intended effects.

Your point of focus is your choice; your thoughts are in your domain. There are two poles to every thought, a negative and a positive. Actively reach toward the positive pole, it will feel like a better feeling thought. The more you play and tip the scales to the positive optimistic view the more you strengthen your muscle of positive faith. Thought by thought as you keep reaching for relief you are being transformed.

You are a very powerful, energetic being. You have a navigational system to help you cross to where you want to go. You have the ability impact to positively impact your life when you pay attention to your feelings and act on your preference to reach for relief. You have power to change beliefs and thereby the whole auto-operating program of your life. It's time to get into the driver's seat and be the navigator you are.

WHAT YOU ARE THINKING IS MAKING YOU FEEL

Our life is what our thoughts make it. – Marcus Aurelius

Be aware of how your thoughts make you feel. You do not have to be a victim to your thoughts; a thought held for over a ¼ minute becomes a feeling. You can actively choose a new view. Begin to recognize when your thoughts are taking you away from your goal.

Some may feel that thoughts cannot be controlled; that they just pop into your head. When you think a thought over and over again, it becomes easier and easier to hold the thoughts for longer and longer. The control starts with your awareness of how you feel in response to automatic thought reactions and how you move your focus to better feeling thoughts. Be aware of how each thought feels and use your focus to expand your possibilities. Improve your point of attraction. By simply focusing on the positive contrast for 15 seconds you will shift into gear.

In the moment to moment, feel better by reaching for relief in choosing better feeling thoughts. When you feel better, you know you have won. It's in getting from here to there that all the interesting things in life happen. Your fulfillment lies in the creative way you design the path bridging the difference to your desires.

FEEL YOUR WAY FORWARD

The definition of insanity is doing the same thing over and over and expecting different results. – Albert Einstein

Focus on your emotions and feel your way to your future reality. Let go of resistance. Let the good flow by being the cause of your intended effect. We need to change how we view/respond to life. Try to deliberately look at the positive. Play virtual reality, and every day as you step through your door into the world, see yourself as the cause you intend to effect. Put on your Wonder Woman Cape and feel ready to take on the world like the queen you are. It is time to rule!

Frame the next segment of your day, before you start a new activity see it going well. Set yourself up so that what comes next is good. Grow your power by directing your thought to the positive. Hold the positive thought for 15 consecutive seconds. Good on you, know you are building your muscles of faith in a bright future. Allow yourself to be positively playful. You have the ability to put your life in a sweet frame. You are up to your problems and know that they will be solved. Have enthusiastic faith.

Crazy or insane can be defined as doing the same thing

and expecting a different result. If you want to feel better or have a different life you need to start to think differently, act differently, believe differently, and feel differently. Create the space to receive the ideas to believe in. Let your emotions guide you; your number one goal is to feel good. So, whatever feels good, go with it: please do your best, to act with respect, to your highest good.

HARNESS POWER

Change your thoughts, change your life. – James Allen

Remember, 80% of success is showing up. Stop the constant auto narrating and show up for Y.O.U., again and again. Help Y.O.U. make the transition from where you are ,to where you want to be. Success = living your life in your own way, thriving along your natural lines of growth.

Study how you came to be where you currently are. You take in information, give meaning to that information, and establish patterns of response which you call upon when you face similar situations. You are now empowered to change the patterns of behavior, that no longer serve you.

Everything is a choice based on evidence gathered and filtered through perceptions and beliefs held as truth. Start to be flexible around the response you are getting. Know you are always more than you think you are. You are a powerful, energetic being, a flexible navigator.

CONSTRUCTING THE REALITY OF Y.O.U.

*When love and skill work together expect a masterpiece. –
John Ruskin*

We all construct our reality. Life as we know it is a construction of memories and information we have gathered along the way. Memories consist of images, sounds and feelings.

The subconscious mind has infinite capacity, it seamlessly runs the body, but something is always programming it. A lot of the time in is not Y.O.U. doing the programming due to information inundation.

Our current program is a collection of everything we have distilled to be true since the beginning of our life. We are constantly constructing a map of how to navigate our way in life. Now our goal is to establish a space of emotional safety as we attempt to do good work in the world.

Be compassionate with yourself. Look at yourself and say: 'I have done the best I know how to do with the resources I have available'. Instead of condemnation be grateful to Y.O.U. Appreciate what you have been able to make up about the world and the strategies you have enacted to navigate your way through it. Have incredible allowance for the diversity that you are. Stay wonderfully Y.O.U.

BE WHAT YOU SEEK

Common sense is the knack of seeing things as they are, and doing things as they ought to be done. – John Billings

To deliberately create, you direct your thoughts, with an understanding of the direct correlation to the feelings they trigger. Now is the best time to be the cause you seek, it is foolish to look to the past for better times for those time are no more.

Our personal preferences are what defines us as individuals. Your preferences are Y.O.U: Your own uniqueness. Your preferences are born through contrast. Pay close attention to the areas you are dissatisfied with. In your dissatisfaction, you are presented with a clarifying opportunity to define what your preference is.

Align your thoughts and feelings with your freedom of present choice. Then consciously choose. Contrast births desire and discord until we attain the desire. It is best to follow the course of your preference as this is your natural line of growth.

This process: contrast, desire, discord, attainment, spirals throughout life, again and again.. We must refocus as we reach new vantage points as our preference system is set again along our natural lines of growth. We succeed by consciously managing the alignment between our thoughts and feelings.

There is nothing like the feeling of a burning desire being thrust to the forefront of our minds. This is our driving force, the best of life, the fuel that propels us. So seek and enjoy the birth on new desires. Your desire enlivens Y.O.U. and Y.O.U. leads to fulfillment.

Use your emotions as a guide to understand how in tune you are with Y.O.U. Pay close attention to your emotions. Are they in harmony with your desire? You can literally feel your way to good. When you allow Y.O.U., you are in alignment with the flow of life.

COME HOME ANY TIME

Great oaks from little acorns grow. – Proverb

Contrast yields meaning. Throughout your life, from birth to death, your mind is always reaching for what it does not yet possess. Therefore happiness will always be around the bend; in sight but just out of reach. Life is never complete, no matter how much we possess there will be something else to desire.

There is a warm fuzzy place within you; this is the place where you are soothed. Perhaps you feel it when you drift off to sleep, or the first glorious blast of warm water in your morning shower, or you feel it when you are sitting at the beach. This is the power we want you to align with. The connection to the excellence of Y.O.U. is critical.

The best way to access the power within you is to believe in Y.O.U.. Others will believe in you only if you believe in yourself. The moment you cease to cherish the vision of a bright future, life loses its shimmer. Lasting fulfillment is what you feel in the pursuit of an unattained objective. Anticipation is a sweet elixir. Have enthusiastic faith in the process of the subconscious mind. After all, you trust it enough to beat your heart.

REINFORCE Y.O.U.

Nothing is impossible to a willing heart. – John Keywood

Tune into yourself

Get to know yourself again: Write down those things that you are passionate about. List your gifts/talents. List your personality characteristics.

Auto-write the real deal

Auto-write for 45 seconds, by answering the questions who am I? Just put your pen to paper and write, don't think, don't pause, just write. Read what you wrote and see where you are at this moment. Remember you are the cause of your effect. Now write: who will I be?

Thought gifting

A powerful gift you can give another is in thought gifting. See something higher and unlimited, in your thoughts for them. You can build an unconscious rapport. Value and listen to other people, look in their eyes and thank them, send them a blessing. Then be the most present person in the room and really listen to them on an energetic level. People that orbit your life will be affected by your thought gifting.

The nifty fifty

Write a list of 50 things you would like have, be, or do

in this life. Reach for 50. Give yourself a break. You may find you peter out somewhere along the way. Keep chipping away at it each day until you have 50. Then begin to review this list quarterly, you will be amazed at the speed in which you begin to check things off!

Seven charms: whole, perfect, strong, powerful, loving, harmonious, happy.

These words are like a magic charm of Y.O.U., your subconscious is soothed and enticed by these words. When focused on often enough the subconscious begins to build a sustainable blueprint of being.

PART III: ENGAGING THRIVE DRIVE

YOUR HEART LEADS YOU TO REACH

Optimism is the faith that leads to achievement. Nothing can be done without hope or confidence. – Helen Keller

Your natural line of vision is toward your horizon, you can create your own personal sunrise by living in the feeling of what you want. Ask for what you need, and intentionally make the way – your mind is problem solving machine.

Step into the rhythm of happiness. Listen to your heart. Come from what you want. Get to know yourself like never before. With the Thrive Drive of Y.O.U. enlivened, life takes on a sense of purpose. You are no longer aimless, but have a definite destination.

In every second of everyday we are making choices; this is the basis of free will. Things in motions tend to say in motion; things at rest tend to stay at rest. Let's get into motion.

We are going to fall into lower frequencies. It is all about how quickly we navigate a return to our natural lines of growth. Reach for what feels good. Relief is only a choice away. Reach for relief and grab it.

MASTER FEAR

Life shrinks or expands in proportion to one's courage. – Anais Nin

Fear abounds throughout life. The most common fears are fear of: poverty, bad health, old age, criticism, loss of love, death. Many times our fears are just scary illusions. Take a second to appreciate your soap- opera masterpiece and then posthaste, recognize it as a big lie.

Grab each fear and examine it. When you are bombarded with thoughts that you are not worthwhile say; 'Ah-Ha, There's that lying thief again.' and release that elusive soul-sucking thought. Good on you, you have hunted down a source of your suffering that has been blocking you from getting what you want.

To stop suffering, it is necessary for you to change your negative thought patterns. When you face difficult times look at them as contrast opportunities to help you get clear on what you really want. Rally your latent forces with mindfulness, meditation and leading questions.

You can deliberately create the life that you want. When you pinpoint your focus you put the power back into your life. First get control of your thoughts to get a hold of your feelings. Begin to focus in 15 second shifts. When you are feeling low, ask yourself: 'Wouldn't it be nice if?'....and focus on the positive contrast for 15 seconds. You are building muscle of faith.

APPLY YOUR POWER

Let me tell you the secret that has led me to my goal. My strength lies solely in my tenacity. – Louis Pasteur

When you take control of your focus, you apply your power and move energy. When you move energy you create change. You are blessed with free-will which you can use to consciously design the life you desire.

Use your concentration and begin to direct the show. Stand in your power. Thoughts cloak themselves in emotions, but first come the thought. Recognize the habitual patterns of thoughts that affect your feelings.

We can be whatever we want, we just have to decide. You are what you are today because of the choices you made over many yesterdays. Tomorrow you will be what you are creating today. Emphasize the good in Y.O.U. and others. Think about positive qualities and they will grow.

This is secret of happiness: accept that you have to continually improve your way of thinking and feeling. Always and forever more, when you feel bad reach for the better feeling. Shift consciousness from one feeling to another.

It is only a matter of degrees between two extreme poles. You choose what you emphasize. Consciously make degree shifts along the pole of contrast toward the positive perception.

Improve the quality of your experience. You no longer permit circumstances to dictate how you feel. Attitude is everything; it is your state of mind and feeling.

How you look at the world dictates your attitude. Your attitude dictates your circumstances. It is not what happens to you but how you see it that counts. Is your attitude helping you or hurting you?

NECESSITY, THE MOTHER OF SKILL

In the middle of difficulty lies opportunity. – Albert Einstein

Two major influences that grow the mind are necessity and a desire to create. Through necessity many of the most useful inventions were created. Every defeat teaches a needed lesson if you are willing to learn it. Sound character is built upon overcoming setbacks.

Failure is only transitory defeat and best viewed as a blessing in disguise. It arrests you from your current course and forces you to redirect your efforts along more advantageous pathways. Mistakes are made so we may learn and profit from them.

We cannot find the cause of our effect outside of ourselves; we must accept full responsibility for our life and all its caused effects. Knowledge becomes power only through organization and use. Sound character is built upon overcoming setbacks. Every defeat teaches a needed lesson if you are willing to learn it.

True character is exhibited by the extent we adapt to our environment and accept responsibility of our perception in the face of adversity. Our strength grows from persistently facing our weaknesses.

Experience is a teacher that shows no favorites, her teachings are cold and unsympathetic. In life, victory goes to those who have developed the strength of character, determination and self control to consistently show up on their own behalf.

A key to directing the subconscious mind is concentration. The subconscious mind can be controlled and directed by the conscious (voluntary) mind. Any idea or thought which is held in the mind, has a tendency to transform. Concentration is the key to this process.

IMAGINATION, A MASTER'S WORKSHOP

Go confidently in the direction of your dreams. Live the life you have imagined. – Henry David Thoreau

Imagination is the workshop of the human spirit, the creative power of this life. In order to have definite purpose, self confidence and initiative you first create these qualities in your imagination. You do this by seeing and feeling yourself in possession of them in your mind's eye. Live from the feeling of receiving your aspiration.

Your achievements grow out of organized plans that you create initially in your imagination. First your imagination forms the thought, and then it organizes the thought into ideas and plans. Next, you see the evidence of the transformation of those plans into reality, as you thrive along your natural lines of growth. You have caused your intended effect.

Self confidence is very important to success, as your thoughts either assist or undermine your efforts. We create our future thought by thought. First Let your goals become reality in your imagination, and never doubt, fully vest in attainment of your ideal. Your goal can be translated into reality after you have fashioned it in the master workshop of your imagination.

The selection of a definite goal calls for the use of both imagination and decision. The power of decision grows with use. Prompt decision forces the imagination to create. This gives it more power to increase your capacity to reach future decisions. Adversity and temporary defeat force you to use your imagination, decide, and to act on your decision.

WHEN ALL ELSE FAILS, LAUGH

Do not take life too seriously. You will never get out of it alive.
– Elbert Hubbard

Laugh whenever possible. Laughter is one of the greatest healing agents. Babies laugh hundreds of times a day. Adults laugh very little. I got outdoors and into nature. I forgave my bad days. There will always be those, we all hold both light and shadow.

What's one way you could laugh more every day? However, the best option of all is to have a big ol' belly laugh. Try to laugh whenever possible, especially at yourself. Envision a baby laughing, feel that giddy joy burgeoning in your chest.Laughter is one of the greatest healing agents.

Studies have shown that babies laugh hundreds of times a day, but adults laugh very little. There is even a yogic practice where you just make yourself laugh. Give it a try: just laugh, pretend if you have to. You just moved energy and raised your vibration, good on you, really.

LEADING QUESTIONS TO CREATE YOUR LIFE YOUR WAY

Begin with the end in mind. – Stephen Covey

You have a problem-solving mind. It will endeavor to solve any problem you throw its way. Use your amazing power to ask better questions. Every thought begins with a question, so why not control the process? You can start to lead your mind to solve your life's problems with Leading Questions.

It is good to get into the habit of asking them every day. You can ask Leading Questions at any time. Center your questions around good vibrations like: vibrant health, success, love, kindness, abundance, joy, strength, or connection.

3 Leading Questions:
- How can I ...?
- What will I do that...?
- Wouldn't it be nice if...?

Example:
- How can I be happy today?
- What will I do that I am happy today?
- Wouldn't it be great if I am happy today?

Ask Leading questions of your problem solving mind to lead Y.O.U. to your goal.

LEADING QUESTIONS WORK FOR Y.O.U.

What lies behind us and what lies before us are tiny matters compared to what lies within us. – Ralph Waldo Emerson

- By asking "How can I...?" you engage your mind to provide you with tangible steps.
- Through inquiring "What will I do that...?" Your mind will look to provide concrete answers to yield your sought-after result.
- Give your subconscious something constructive to work on. Activate your imagination by asking "Wouldn't it be great if....?"

Ask your limitless mind all your questions, and then trust in faith, not fear. Open your heart. Believe in the possibilities of Y.O.U.. Be optimistic in that infinite energy that beats your heart. Only lack of confidence will obstruct you. Have wonderful dreams and believe they will come true.

You will always find what you are looking for whether it is good or bad. Seek the good. Think about your positive qualities and they will grow. Accept that you have to continually improve your way of thinking and feeling.

GET ENTHUSED

One can succeed at almost anything for which he has unlimited enthusiasm. – Charles M. Schwab

Enthusiasm is a state of mind when you are stimulated and inspired to act on your aim. Enthusiasm is contagious and affects all it comes in contact with. Fuel your life with enthusiasm for your aspiration in life. Be enthusiastic about it now. Share your enthusiasm and become a dynamic person which others are drawn to.

Your enthusiasm is a vital force that impels action and inspires others. Mix enthusiasm into your everyday to stay energized. All you interact with will benefit from your positive expectancy.

Your state of mind becomes obvious to all who hear you by the tone of your voice. Use this tool often; put enthusiasm into your tone of voice. Infuse your attitude with enthusiasm. No words can replace the tone of voice from a deep belief backed by unyielding enthusiasm.

Enthusiasm urges you to put your knowledge into action. Become intoxicated on your enthusiasm and then do your work with love in your heart. The effect will be masterful and you will enjoy the process of creating it.

Happiness is the final object of all our efforts, it is a state of mind that is maintained by anticipation of future achievement. It is wonderful to happily dream of heights of achievement that are yet attained with enthusiastic faith. Faith is one of the greatest powers on earth it offers peace to those that embrace it.

POSITIVE CONSTRUCTIVE THOUGHTS

Two roads diverged in a wood, and I took the one less traveled by, and that has made all the difference. – Robert Frost

Without a doubt your dominating thoughts will manifest the reality of your life, success or failure is defined in the nature of your thoughts. Most human misery stems from lack of self control.

Self control boils down to thought control. Thought is your most important tool to fashion your bright future. The key that opens the door to the source of your power is found the moment you learn to control your thoughts.

Stimulus to your brain comes from either outside suggestion or self suggestion. All that happens is recorded in your subconscious mind.

It is so easy in this day of modern conveniences and immediate gratification to be distracted. Thought is the only thing in which you have absolute control. It would be a great shame to let most of your thoughts and actions be simulated from external stimuli.

Place in your mind through self suggestion, the positive constructive thoughts which harmonize with your greatest desire and your mind will transform those thoughts into cause of the effect.

Y.O.U. AND M.E.

The Thrive Drive is an evolutionary stable system 10,000 years in the making which we can leverage for our betterment. It is comprised of Y.O.U and M.E.

Y.O.U. is a supremely intelligent highly responsive automated machine. M.E. is the muscle, the means to enacting your divine design. M.E. is your feet on the street, You see, Your Own Uniqueness needs My Excellence to heed its call and bring it's impetus to life.

Listen, it's all about Y.O.U. Your own uniqueness, the seed of excellence you came programmed with. Like a tiny acorn destined to be a great oak. You have a divine design, an amazing light of your own uniqueness to shine.

Your Navigator directs you to flow along your natural lines of growth with ease by steadfastly pointing toward your true north. The Navigator of Y.O.U. signals through your internal compass which we interpret as feelings of resistance or flow.

We all seek harmonious flow in our lives. Everybody has their own flow of divine design. AND it's your job to figure out where your flow is and how to access it. In developing Thrive Drive skills you play the role of both student and teacher as you learn from yourself. It's a mastery thing and you will practice getting better at self-awareness for a life time.

DELIBERATELY CHOOSE

Far away there in the sunshine are my highest aspirations. I may not reach them but I can look up and see their beauty, believe in them, and try to follow where they lead. – Louisa May

When you deliberately choose the thoughts that dominate your mind and firmly refuse to admit outside suggestion, you are exercising the highest form of self control.

This power of thought control is a gift given solely to man. Exercise it well and be blessed with a rich life. Keep in mind, first came the thought then the thing.

A strong desire to be transformed into reality must be backed with persistency that knows no defeat until it is taken as truth by the subconscious mind.

Stimulate your mind with a strong deeply seated desire so that the powers of the mind will function constructively Desire is seed of all achievement.

THE GREATEST DISCOVERY OF ALL

Destiny is not a matter of chance. It is a matter of choice. It is not something to be waited for. But rather something to be achieved. – William Jennings Bryan

Great discovery is always self discovery; the truth we are all seeking is wrapped up in Y.O.U. You are the master of your fate. You captain your course when you control your own thoughts. Guard your thoughts more carefully than you would guard your most valuable possessions.

The power to think as you wish is the only power over which you have absolute control. It is within your power to control your thoughts. The responsibility rests squarely upon your shoulders whether your thoughts are positive or negative. Think thoughts of a positive, expectant nature and watch your thoughts create these conditions.

Concentration now becomes a key to your success. To concentrate is to focus the mind. Focus on a given desire until ways and means for its realization have been worked out successfully by your subconscious. These plans then will be put into operation.

Suggestion and habit are two the most important

influences on concentration. Focus on your desire often. Breathe life into it. See it real in your heart. Let it beat its rhythm into life.

CONFIDENTLY STEP OUT

We are what we repeatedly do. Excellence, then, is not an act, but a habit. – Aristotle

Believe in attaining your aspiration. Then proceed ahead without fear, without doubt. Habit is the map which the mental path follows. To transform a goal into physical reality hold it in your conscious mind faithfully. Persistently suggest to subconscious mind until habit begins to give it permanent form.

Bear in mind that every word spoken within your hearing, every sight that reaches your eyes, every sense impression you receive through the five senses, influences your subconscious as surely as the sun rises in the east and sets in the west.

Each time you fail you have the choice to go down in permanent defeat or rise with renewed energy. You attain in proportion to how you interpret your past experience and use those experiences as a basis of working plans. Failure is just nature's way of preparing you for your greatness.

MASTER FORTUNE

Our deepest fear is not that we are inadequate. Our deepest fear is that we are powerful beyond measure. – Marianne Williamson

It is through the medium of thought that we become masters of our fortune. The fact is that you are the maker of your own lot in life. Your thoughts and acts are the tools with which you do the making.

Every thought you release changes your character in exact accordance. You are punishing yourself with every wrong you commit and rewarding yourself with every constructive act.

Think of others as you would want them to think of you. Your positive thought will develop your dynamic personality. Try to be tolerant with other and easily allow as you live and let live.

Interact with others as you would wish them to do unto you. You reap what you sow. Know the results of every thought you think are returned to you.

FEAR'S ILLUSION

The only thing we have to fear is fear itself. – Franklin D. Roosevelt

The struggle to scrap out a stable existence in these harried materialistic times is immense, it is easy to drift aimlessly through life. Realize that disuse brings only atrophy and decay, strength and growth come only through continuous effort. Your mind develops from and grows through the law of use. Nature hates a void and in her realm idleness leads to waste.

Mental inertia is so common these days and the scary thing is stagnant minds are the breeding place of fear. Our most dangerous enemy is fear. The main underlying fear is the fear of death. Fear has six basic faces: Fear of Poverty, Fear of Death, Fear of Ill Health, Fear of the Loss of Love, Fear of Old Age, Fear of Criticism. The key here is unlocking fears illusion.

It is of critical importance to learn to organize and direct your natural talents toward a definite purpose. Your mind once stimulated by a strong desire becomes a harnessed power. Your actions reflect your dominating thoughts thus Singleness of purpose is essential for success. You are now engaged in training for success by keeping a well organized, alert and energetic mind in the daily trials of life.

You can acquire everything you need to attain your goal by organizing all your knowledge. Develop that knowledge into power that bridges all your weaknesses.

AARRCC INTO Y.O.U.

Don't go through life, grow through life. – Eric Butterworth

It's time to manage your mind. Condition your mind to the positive shift you are consciously making. A simple process that will help get you bridge from here to there is call **AARRCC** short for Appreciative Awareness, Realigning Recognition and Charging Change.

Let's break down the pieces.

Appreciative Awareness:

Start by actually arcing as in sit up nice and tall, love your posture. Bring your shoulders to your ears and drop them. Lift your chest as if a string were pulling up your chest.

Breathe life: breath slow and low and know you are breathing the stuff of life with each breath. Be appreciative of the masterful reality you have created, really you are a master creator.

Realigning Recognition

Be aware that you have the ability to direct your focus and make a better choice.

Root yourself to the earth by envisioning a you connecting right down to the center of the earth, feel safe and connected to all that is. Practice 20 kegels to reaffirm the connection in your root energy center.

Say some Ho'oponopono: I love you I am sorry Please forgive me Thank you. Say these statements for yourself and then as you feel inclined dedicate them to others.

Charging Change

Breath up into the sun and feel yourself connecting up to its loving bright light full of inspiration. Ask some leading questions: How can I ? What will I do that? Wouldn't it be nice if....

Look at a statement proclaiming your worth. (ie. I am worthy of being vibrantly healthy). Close your eyes, see the statement & feel the effect result. Open read the statement. Close your eyes see the statement feel the result/effect. Do this five or more times. You are increasing your rate of transformation!

CAUSE IN EFFECT

Knowing is not enough we must apply. Willing is not enough; we must do – Johann Wolfang von Goethe

To be the cause of your effect you must be from what it is you seek. To be what you seek you must align with Your Own Uniqueness. Y.O.U. unlocks your internal compass which leads you to where you want to be.

The trick is to know how to enliven your own uniqueness to a level where you feel it engaged in your life. It has an energy flow that is optimal for you to thrive. Our goal is to automate you being at an optimal set point and consistently sending out the right cause vibration, so you can hold right focus to draw forth the effect you seek.

So that no matter what you are facing, no matter how hard things appear right now. You are always have the power to focus your cause effect and improve the circumstance...

When you are aligned with the Thrive Drive of Y.O.U. it acts as a powerful signal drawing to you what you are being the cause of. It is the secret of this technique that entrains your feeling set point higher and higher...so you feel better and better and more good returns to your life.

So when you awaken your solar plexus you can literally magnetize massive transformation and abundance to you. Once your Thrive Drive is Automated you just feel better and everything looks brighter…

IT'S A MASTERY THING – WE WILL PRACTICE FOR A LIFETIME

Winners never quit and quitters never win! – Vince Lombardi

We will dance with meeting ourselves on the road again and again in the spiral dance of learning. You will practice and remember and then forget and then remind yourself not to forget. Practice until this learning is instinctual and then the good begins to flow in faster and faster.

Focus on harmony and alignment. Breathe into these vibrant color centers, know you are taking the stuff of life directly to the center and letting the good flow. Just breathe low and slow, all the truth to seep in as you see and breathe that color, spin it clockwise. Enjoy the connection to creating cause.

Balance your energy centers by being aware of the feeling of centered truth harmonizing you. Center truth that feels challenged by daily stress can now be focused on with love, soothed, balanced and aligned to innovate out of any problem. These techniques can be used in everyday life. Practice, if you recognize yourself in opposition to a center truth, work with balancing that center. Breathe chi bring the center the energy of life.

The goal is to consistently balance your center truths so your energy system is running smoothly avoiding traffic jams that lead to dis-ease.

PART IV: FLIP ON THE POWER SWITCH

PLANT A SEED FOR TOMORROW WISELY

A journey of a thousand miles begins with a single step. – Confucius

Systems of allowing help you move through life with minimum resistance and friction. Success is the power to manifest what you intend in life. Power is the organized effort that builds the foundation of abundance from the organization of facts, knowledge and capabilities. When you live in your power you radiate confidence as you understand and apply organized effort in the attainment of your goals.

Your mind is both broadcasting and receiving thought vibrations. The subconscious mind is like a magnet, and when it is vitalized and inundated with a passionate desire, it attracts all that is necessary for its fulfillment.

Your primary aim in life needs to be backed by a burning desire for its attainment. Desire is the factor which determines Y.O.U and what your excellence in life shall be; no one can select this desire but you. Select your principal aspiration with care and let it bring you happiness, peace and prosperity that endure.

HAPPILY FILL FREE TIME

The best way to predict the future is to create it. – Peter F. Drucker

Until you select a definite purpose in life you dissipate your energies. Weakness and indecision ensue. When you organize your faculties and direct them toward the attainment of a definite purpose you take advantage of developing the power of organized effort.

By constantly keeping in mind precisely what you want your desire becomes like a magnifying glass under direct sun, able to start a fire. Concentrate your attention on a given task until completed and you will strengthen the blueprint of your future success.

Enjoy imagining achieving a great aim. Imagine it every day, ask/intend for it, visualize yourself attaining it, and expect it with enthusiastic faith. Come from feeling state of attaining it now.

Make that aim clear, believe you can achieve it and back it up with a persistence which does not recognize the word impossible. Have fun with it, having a burning desire is invigorating. The object of your aim should become your hobby, something that happily fills your free time.

KEEP AN OPEN MIND

Minds are like parachutes they only function when they are open. – Thomas Dewar

Skepticism is the enemy of self development. Thought is the most highly organized form of energy. Fear is the main reason for unhappiness and despair. The key to open the door to success and happiness is to master the fear that whispers in your ear that you cannot do it. The players in the game of life boldly step to the front. Fear keeps many spectators in back row wondering what other may say.

We are always suggesting to ourselves, whether they be good or bad. It is an established fact that the faculties of the mind, like the limbs of the body, atrophy and wither away from disuse. Self confidence is no exception, it is developed by use or it disappears.

Inaction leads to atrophy thus ambition and self confidence are essential qualities do combat complacency. Struggle is not a disadvantage but an advantage as it develops qualities in us that may have lain dormant without strife to awaken them. To be forced by circumstance to do your best breeds temperance, self control, and strength. By overcoming struggle you become persistent and persistence is worth much more than money.

A PLAN TO DIRECT YOUR EFFORTS

Shoot for the moon. Even if you miss, you'll land among the stars. – Les Brown

Your mind is like a battery that can be positively or negatively charged; self confidence is a quality by which the mind is positively charged. You can succeed by deliberately charging your mind with sufficient self confidence to make your mind an irresistible force.

Any idea firmly fixed in your subconscious mind, by repeated thought over and over again, automatically becomes a plan directing your efforts toward its attainment.

Believe in yourself and back this belief with a dynamic, aggressive action that leads all to know of your belief and self reliance. Self confidence is contagious, it is impelling, it is persuasive, it attracts others and the results you seek.

To be successful in living of life you must be able to change the color of your mind. You will resemble, tomorrow the dominating thoughts of your mind today. Plant a seed for tomorrow wisely.

HAVE FUN, PLAY WITH CHOICE

Life isn't about finding yourself. Life is about creating yourself. – George Bernard Shaw

Your preference is your guide in this life. Your preference is designed choice by choice to bring you into alignment with your natural lines of growth. These natural lines of growth lead you to the excellence only you can share.

You were born therefore you have value. Believe you have something wonderful to share. When you feel excited about something know you are working in the arena of your dreams.

Begin to add choice to your daily routine and play with your options. Have some fun going with your unique preference. Let yourself feel free to decide.

As you stay more positive each day, your passions will stir. Your enthusiasm will gain momentum. New horizons open up as you follow your interests to discover what you desire most in life.

The process is simple: in the moment ask, "What is my preference here? What would my heart say? Which feels better?" Then trust, decide and act. Everyday will be an opportunity to enhance your state of mind.

PURPOSEFUL PASSION GLITTERING ON YOUR HORIZON

Watch your thoughts; they become words. Watch you words; they become actions. Watch your actions; they become habits. Watch your habits; they become character. Watch your character; it becomes your destiny. – Frank Outlaw

Your purposeful passion will become defined, preference by preference, glittering on the horizon, beckoning you forward. You now have a destination in life, a map to gain your bearings whenever you feel lost.

As you start to name your desire, intend to devote time daily to acquiring it. An insightful shortcut to your desired goal is learning about who you most admire and understanding why.

You receive an abundance of what you ask for, so really get clear on what it is you want. Come from a place that you are enough and believe it. Train you mind to seek abundance rather than lack and limitation.

Look for the wonders that are present in every day of your life, give thanks. Appreciate, be grateful for what you have created, and laugh joyfully at how masterful you are.

WEIGHT THE SCALES OF YOUR DAY MORE POSITIVELY

Do what you can, with what you have, where you are. – Theodore Roosevelt

We are stocking our personal tool box to be best equipped to master our lives. First, we must master our time. Each day firmly weight the scales of fortune to the positive side. To make the future we want tomorrow the majority of our time today has to be filled with creating instead of tearing down.

Give yourself more choices and begin to make better decisions. You are putting mechanisms in place to shield yourself from negative influences and self-defeating patterns.

You can begin to use suggestion to influence your life just by focusing on the good stuff. Simply, think of what you want instead of what you don't. You can take your life where you want it to go. Get psyched.

Let's do the math: 24 hours make up 100% of your day.

Imagine two scales counter balancing each other, one side positive and the other negative, measuring the use of your time. Your goal is to tip the scales of time to the positive, but you don't want to just tip them, you want to slam dunk it.

If you make the last thought before sleep a good one, you will reprogram your subconscious mind positively during sleep. You will begin your day 33% positive. Thought by thought, decision by decision, action by action, you will tilt the percentages of fortune in your favor. You are updating your belief system.

FEEL THE SUN

The mind is not a vessel to be filled but a fire to be kindled. – Plutarch

One wonderful way to really feel amazing is to close your eyes and think of the blazing sun. See the sun shining brightly, blinding with its intensity. Feel its warmth on your face. Then, allow in your mind's eye your energy to merge with that of the sun.

Become one with the sun, feel the power seeping into all that you are, filling you up with pure light. Get your fill of the power, plug in. Shine down on all you love. See them raise their heads to take in your brilliant light and warmth. Share with the world your shining glory.

TAKE A LOAD OFF

Love conquers all. – Virgil

Take a huge load off your shoulders. Look at where you can forgive in your life. Holding on to anger and past hurt only hurts you. It blocks your vital energy from flowing freely.

A practice of forgiveness that is very easy and wonderfully rewarding is just four simple phrases. Say them in any order you prefer: 'I love you, I am sorry, please forgive me, thank you.' I understand this is called Ho'oponopono and is an ancient Hawaiian practice that clears old programming, helps you forgive, and plain makes you feel better.

You can use this peaceful practice in any number of ways. Say the phrases over and over, in song, whispered under your breath, silently in your head, or aloud as is a prayer. You can offer it to yourself or dedicate it to someone you love or a cause you feel strongly about. Good on you.

YOU'VE GOT THE POWER

The difference, between the impossible and the possible lies in a person's determination. – Tommy Lasorda

The more you play and tip the scales to the positive, an optimistic view the more you receive wins. There are two powerful times to help tip the scales of time positive to your favor:
1. the first 45 minutes in the morning is a powerful gratitude compounder, spend some time here appreciating what you have and focusing on what you want coming from a place of gratitude.
2. The second is the last thought before sleep, make it a good on and set yourself to arise weighted 33% to the positive.

You are a very powerful energetic being you have a navigation system to help you bridge to where you want to go. You have the ability impact life to the positive by paying attention to your feelings and then acting on your preference to reach for relief. Now have power to change beliefs.

USE POWERFUL OF LANGUAGE

You have to expect things of yourself before you can do them.
– Michael Jordan

Words hold so much power. Words can have a positive or negative effect. Delete powerless words from your language.

Do not try, or hope, or want. Instead intend and be. Start saying, "I intend that…" and "I am…" These will make the way forward easier.

We have to stop shoulding on ourselves. Instead of wishing, wanting, hoping, shoulding, having to, needing to; begin now to:

- Intend
- Be in process of
- Decide to

The more you play with the power of language the better you will get.

DREAM IT UP

Hold fast to dreams, for if dreams die, life is broken winged bird that cannot fly. – Langston Hughes

Engage that imagination of yours. Visualization helps you to just engage your imagination. Allow yourself to go with your imagination, permit the suggestion. Relax and accept the story. Like reading a good book, get wrapped up and give yourself over to the feeling.

Visualization is a relaxed state, engaging imaginations, it's like exercises for your mind. Build rapport with your unconscious mind.

Continually ask yourself:
- What would it look like to achieve my goal?
- What would a picture of it look like?
- How would it feel?

BREATHE LIFE

Our aspirations are our possibilities. – Robert Browning

Breath aids in all things. It helps you get present quickly. There are so many ways to work with breath. Here are just a few:

- To inhale well first you must exhale. Breathe out the toxins, think Darth Vader, and breathe out all the way. Get the junk out of the bottom of your lungs.
- Deep diaphragmatic breathing is a great way to connect you into the moment. You can follow the breath on its journey through your body. See it entering your nose, moving down your throat into your belly, going deep in your lungs, feeding your body the stuff of life, nourishing you, healing you. Watch it leave, taking with it all your stress, toxins, disease and fear.
- Breathe slow and low. Fill your lungs bottom up. Enjoy connecting with prana. Chi, the stuff of life is in each breath.
- Become conscious of your breath going in and out. Try to use and feel all of your lungs, from down deep in your belly up to your throat.

Breathe in light and move it through your body with your breath.

BREATH WORKS FOR Y.O.U.

Know thyself. – Socrates

- Breathe in and think, "I am calm." Breathe out and think, "I smile." Breathe with loved ones of the past and present. You can breathe with your ancestors. Meditate while you walk and mindfully breathe in for a certain number of steps and exhale for the same amount of steps. Walk into the present moment gracefully like a lion or an elephant.
- Try the chill-out breath. Breathe out and then breathe in for a count of 5 and then breathe out for a count of six. You will find a sense of calm growing.
- Get centered and focused. Try triangular breathing. Simply breathe in for a count of 4, hold for a count of 4 and breathe out for a count of 4.
- Stand in your power and energize. Try square breathing:, just add one more side on your triangle. Breathe in for a count of 4, hold for a count of 4, breathe out for a count of 4 and hold

for count of 4.
- Breathe out Fear. Breathe in through your nose, "I breathe in Peace." Breathe out through mouth, "I breathe out Fire."
- Feel safe and secure. "So Hung" loosely interpreted means "My identity is infinite." Breathe in through your nose "So." Breathe out through your mouth "Hung."

PART V: ENERGY LIFE MAP

WORKING ENERGY

We must be the change we wish to see. – Mahatma Gandhi

Life is no easy mistress. She deals blows without warning. Her blows give you the opportunity to start again. The energy that brings us into life is the energy that animates our bodies and keeps us alive. There are many ways to tap into this energy. Let the power of energy get you giddy with excitement because you have access to it. You can rally it to aid you in your endeavors. You have access to tremendous resources.

Energy is the vital life force. It is that which distinguishes life from death. It is this energy that nourishes the cells of our body. Energy has an anatomy that it moves throughout your body. There are centers along this anatomy that are hubs, energy portals in and out of your physical body to the environment.

There are things that disrupt the flow of energy by creating dis-ease or disease. Dis-ease can be caused by stress in its many forms, stuffed unexpressed emotions, how you visualize yourself, and your internal dialogue habits thoughtlessly created in childhood now rule and are not serving your highest good.

Using the tools outlined below you can begin going in

a new direction. You are the one who could make all the difference. Discover the power of your focus. Your thoughts hold energy. You have a choice: you can choose a better way to speak to yourself and see yourself better. What to learn more on your energy map? Check out your free gifts and learn about a deep dive workshop www.faceforwardyou.com/thrive-guide-gifts.

THE SEVEN ENERGY CENTERS

Success leaves clues. – Jim Rohn

The energy centers also called Centers. Each energy center holds a life lesson necessary to understand for proper use of our free will.

Energy flows in and out of everyone through their Centers. The literal translation of Center is wheel. They are the personal portals to the flow of the body. Centers are spinning wheels of energy located in 7 primary areas of the body. Centers must be balanced or life is unbalanced.

There are seven main Centers along your torso that keep the energy balanced throughout your body. They are located along your body in a vertical line from the groin to the top of the head. The seven Centers are: the groin Center, the navel Center, the solar plexus Center, the heart Center, the throat Center, the third eye Center and the crown Center. Each Center has truths to understand, lessons to learn and expressions to share. When the Centers are not expressed the energy does not flow correctly throughout your body, or in and out from the universe.

They move up in the colors of the rainbow, ROYGBIV:

at the groin is the red Center of connection to tribe; above is the navel Center, orange, representing our ability to create; right below your chest plate is your personal power Center, yellow in its fierce burning will. The green Center is your heart Center, balancing your power with compassion and love. Your throat holds your blue Center of expression. Between your eyes is the third eye, a beautiful indigo of intuition and guidance. The crown Center is violet and holds the connection to all, understanding I am that I am.

Let us take a journey through the energy centers for a better sense of what areas of interest of each Center and how they impact our life. As you get to know your center truths try to look at the expression of the opposite of the truth in your life.

It is in the place we do not want that we find what we want. What I mean is know with compassionate observation you will notice when you hold yourself in a space of opposition to a center truth. When you hold space in opposition you will feel dis-ease as energy get blocked in its flow throughout its system. Remember again to be gentle with yourself and do not judge just take note and be open to receiving relief.

For the first center I give you an example of an opposition to the center truth. This I do not continue for it is a personal story and we should each hear our voice narrating our story.

The tools provided to soothe the opposition are easy and fun. You can now make perfume with scents that speak to your center truths seeking expression. With color you can dress to express your truth authentically each day. Gemstones can make your life sparkle as you show representation of earth in center truth there by resounding.

You can work directly to move stagnant old stuffed emotions that are blocking your brilliant shine. This center truth work is powerfully attractive in amplifying your best life to you now. Keep an open mind and try some of the visualizations on the grocery line.

R

ROOT CENTER

Root Center Location: Base of spine

Root Center Concept: WHOLE

Root Center Truths:
- The Right to Life, Instinct, the Will to live
- All is One, Connected to earth, Connected to all
- Rooted to earth in this life here and now
- Security, order, can take care of self

Root Center Lessons:
- Survival of the individual
- Tribal mind, family, group belief patterns
- Self preservation, survival instincts
- Strength to stand up for one's self

Root Center Expressions:
- Physical Attraction
- Grounded in our activities
- Code of honor, familial bonds
- Treat others as want to be treated
- Ability to manifest dreams

Balance Root Center:
- Color: Red

- Aromatherapy Scents: Patchouli, Sandalwood, Cedar wood, Myrrh, Thyme, Musk, Pine, Magnolia,
- Gemstones: Black Onyx, Bloodstone, Carnelian, Garnet, Labradorite, Ruby
- Massage: Base of spine, Little finger or little toe
- Sit on earth, watch sunrise/sunset
- Kegel exercises
- Meditation visualization: Red wheel of light spinning
- Chant: LAM

NAVEL CENTER

Navel Center Location: Navel
Navel Center Concept: PERFECT
Navel Center Truths:
- Honor one another
- Right to create
- Survival of the species
- Inherently Deserve Pleasure, Well Being, Abundance
- Ability to Create

Navel Center Lessons:
- Challenge motivations based on social conditioning
- Partnership
- Sex, power, money, pleasure

Navel Center Expressed:
- Sexual expression for procreation
- Act with honor and integrity in relationships
- Commitment

Balance Navel Center:
- Color: Orange

- Aromatherapy Scents: Jasmine, Rose, Sandalwood, Honeysuckle, Musk
- Gemstones: Citrine, Coral, Agate, Topaz, Rose quartz, Moonstone, opal
- Visualize a wheel of brilliant orange (more brilliant color the higher vibration.
- Chant: VAM
- Relax in body of water, look at moon
- Massage ring finger

SOLAR PLEXUS CENTER

Solar Plexus Center Location: Stomach
Solar Plexus Center Concept: STRONG
Solar Plexus Center Truths:
- Personal power – control over one's life
- Self love and care
- Right to Personal Identity, Self esteem, Self Respect
- Strength

Solar Plexus center Lessons:
- View yourself in relation to others
- Honor yourself, able to stand up on your own, Self worth
- Each is responsible for the quality of person one becomes

Solar Plexus center Expressions:
- Assertive action, sharp mind, mastery
- Ego, personality, self expression
- Gut Instincts
- Love our lives are they are now, flaws and all, Be

grateful for life
- Individuation,
- Self confidence

Balance Solar Plexus Center
- Color: Yellow
- Aromatherapy Scents: Bergamot, Vetivert, Ylang Ylang, Clove, Mint
- Gemstones: Amber, Citrine, Howlite, Jasper, Labradorite, Tiger eye, Topaz
- Visualize Wheel of yellow light, 1000 suns in the center of your being
- Being in bright sunlight
- Massage middle finger
- Chant: RAM

HEART CENTER

Heart Center Location: Center of Chest
Heart Center Concept: POWERFUL
Heart Center Truths:
- Right to love, love is divine power
- Attend to self emotional needs
- Compassion

Heart Center Lessons:
- Self love
- Forgiveness
- Ability to express love

Heart center Expressions:
- Nurturing
- Love
- Acceptance
- Express emotions truly
- Devotion, Reverence
- Sympathy

Balance Heart Center:
- Color: Green and pink
- Aromatherapy Scents: Bergamot, Rose, Amber,

Jasmine
- Gemstones: Emerald, Aventurine, Jade, Malachite, Moonstone, Rose quartz, Tourmaline
- Wheel of green or pink light at center of chest
- Massage pointer finger
- Walking in lush green setting, gazing at pink flowers
- Chant: YAM (YA-OM)
- Shoulder rolls

THROAT CENTER

Throat Center Location: Center of neck
Throat Center Concept: LOVING
Throat Center Truths:
- Wisdom
- Commitment to truth, Integrity
- Expression of One's Truth
- The right to personal truth
- Integrity

Throat Center Lessons:
- Consciously recognize own needs
- Surrender your will to the your highest self
- Setting intention
- Following one's truth,
- Dealing with the unknown

Throat Center Expressions:
- Creative Flow, Communication
- Self expression, Will to communicate one's true inner feelings
- Communicate gently, not hurt or judge others
- Negotiation

Balance Throat Center:
- Color: Blue
- Scents: Chamomile, Myrrh, Lilac, Frankincense, Patchouli
- Gemstones: Aquamarine, Azurite, Topaz, Celestite, Pearl, Fluorite, Moonstone
- Visualize Wheel of sky blue at throat
- Chant: HAM
- Massage thumb
- Time outside absorbing the clear blue sky, being near clear blue water
- Lion face: Open mouth wide stick tongue out
- Shrug shoulders, Neck rolls

BROW CENTER

Brow Center Location: Between Eyebrows, third eye
Brow Center Concept: HARMONIOUS
Brow Center Truths:
- Highest good guidance
- Intellect
- Trust you will have what you need when you need it
- Inner knowing
- Peace

Brow Center Lessons:
- Clear lucid thinking
- Seek only truth
- Healthy thinking
- Ability to see within, Introspection
- Evaluate our belief system
- Strive to support and not judge

Brow Center Expressions:
- Discernment
- Imagination
- Wisdom
- Harmony

- Visualization
- Balance Brow Center
- Color: Indigo (dark starry night)
- Aromatherapy Scents: Hyacinth, Rose, Geranium, Violet, Amber, Sandalwood
- Gemstones: Celestite, Clear Quartz, Opal, Sapphire, Lapis Lazuli
- Visualize wheel of indigo blue light at brow
- Gently massage brow
- Chant: OM
- Relax and contemplate the blue starry night sky

CROWN CENTER

Crown Center Location: Top of head

Crown Center Concept: HAPPY

Crown Center Truths:
- I am that I am
- Connection to all
- Inspiration
- Spirit is eternal only the body is temporary

Crown Center Lessons:
- Beyond subject/object
- Deep inner searching, spiritual quest
- Spiritual seeking
- Spirit commands the body

Crown Center Expressions:
- Live in present moment
- Humanitarianism
- Serenity
- Appreciate Beauty

Balance Crown Center:
- Color: Violet or Golden White
- Aromatherapy Scents: Frankincense, Lavender,

Rosewood
- Gemstones: Amethyst, Diamond, Labradorite, Quartz, Iolite, Moldavite, Fluorite
- Visualize a wheel of white light
- Chant: M
- Time alone at top of mountain with magnificence and silence
- Massage top of head

PART VI: COLOR MAGIC

COLOR YOUR LIFE WITH MAGIC

Nothing splendid has ever been achieved except by those who dared to believe that something inside of them was superior to circumstance. – Bruce Barton

When you wear colors you speak to your power. Each color has the potential to bring something different to your day. It may become a pleasure to dress in the morning as you choose what you will say to yourself and other by your choice of colors.

Help yourself to a good dose of color. It will add that little bit of pep to your day that might be otherwise lacking. In addition, by your use of color, you might transmit good vibes to another. The colors you are attracted to reflect who you are, where you are and where you are going.

The colors are tied to our energy centers.
- Red, orange and yellow are warm stimulating colors
- Green is the bridge, both stimulating and peaceful.
- Blue, violet and indigo are calm peaceful colors.

When you are attracted to a color over all colors maybe something is missing in your life, because you are avoiding the other experiences other colors draw. Visualize, use crystals, use colored light, eat and drink colored food, wear color, use colored gemstones.

RED MAGIC

The past does not equal the future. – Anthony Robbins

Red is the color of the first power center, the root chakra, dense and full color. Red ties us to our roots and grounds us in our day. It can be used as a helpful reminder to stake out our ground.

Red is brimming with fun and passion. It helps us feel connected to others. Red is love. Red helps energy manifest physically. Red is the color of luck. Red is an energizer. Red stimulates.

Red is a moving color, it gets you moving. Red gets our attention. Red is a dancing color. Red is sacred goddess energy. Red is creation energy of sex and earth.

The symbol of New York City is a big apple which is red with represents NYC is always moving. Red brings energy to physical form. Use red when you feel flighty. Red will ground you to the earth. Red is a color of stability.

ORANGE MAGIC

Don't ask yourself what the world needs: ask yourself what makes you come alive. And then go and do that. Because what the world needs is people who have come alive. – Harold Whitman

Orange is the color of our second power center located in the naval area. Orange can help us when we need to create something. It can inspire us to create what we want and have the power to present it.

Orange is bursting with life. Orange is associated with joy, warmth, heat, sunshine, enthusiasm, creativity, success, encouragement, change, determination, health, stimulation, happiness, fun, enjoyment, balance, sexuality, freedom, expression, and fascination. Orange is the color of joy and creativity.

YELLOW MAGIC

No one knows what s/he can do until s/he tries. – Publilius Syrus

Yellow is the color of the sun and full of fun. It is color of the third power center located in our solar plexus. It can help you to manifest your power, to have the strength to choose to use your power. Wearing yellow can help you take that idea you had floating around in your head and take the actions necessary to make it a reality.

Yellow is a notice me color a color that says I want to be noticed. When you where it you say I am okay to have people look at me, see me.

Yellow is a color of seeing clearly. Yellow is a thinking energy. The solar plexus Center is a merging point of a lot of energy paths of the body. When meditate take energy in and take it up.

Yellow is the color of the solar plexus Center the center of self esteem and confidence. Yellow is the color of intellect and quiet knowledge.

Yellow is a left brain color it process things and works things out. Yellow helps you wake up and invigorates you. Use yellow when need to get analytical left brain work done. Yellow is harvest energy. Yellow is a happy upbeat color. Yellow is the color of spirit. Yellow is an inspirational color.

GREEN MAGIC

Imagine all the people living life in peace. You may say I'm a dreamer, but I'm not the only one. I hope someday you'll join us, and the world will be as one. – John Lennon

Green is the color of nature, it is bountiful and nurturing. Green is the color of the fourth power center located near our heart. Wearing green can help you love and appreciate yourself.

Green can put love in every step of your day. Let green assist you in forgiving the certain someone or having more patience with the one who usually gets under your skin.

Green is a color that brings balance. The heart center balances the three centers above with the three centers below. Green is a color that gives you space. It reminds you get quiet, inspires you to meditate in nature.

BLUE MAGIC

Seek first to understand, then be understood. – Stephen Covey

Blue is the color of the fifth power center located in your throat. Wearing blue can help you express yourself clearly. Put on blue the day of your big presentation and feel confident that you will be persuasive and speak to the best of your ability.

Wearing blue can also help you feel connected to your inner gumption to be yourself fully. Blue assists keeping you connected to your best self. Blue helps you express yourself authentically.

Blue is the color of expressive creation. Blue is of the throat center which connects sound to vibration. Use sound in meditation (gongs, crystal bowls, chant, japa meditation) to connect to your truth. Blue is a soulful color.

Where blue to interview to represent trustworthiness. Blue is a color of purpose, the mission in life. Blue is like the penicillin of color, if something is wrong try throwing some blue on it.

Blue is the color of peace and calm. Blue is a healing energy. Blue is the color of surprise. Blue is the color of work, wear it to get things done. Blue is the color of acceptance. Blue is for communication, speaking your truth.

INDIGO MAGIC

How far you go in life depends on you being tender with the young, compassionate with the aged, sympathetic with the striving and tolerant of the weak and the strong. Because someday in life you will have been all of these. – George Washington Carver

Indigo is the color of the deep midnight sky. Indigo is the color of our sixth power center located in our brow. When you want to feel inner inspiration, wearing indigo will be a good place to start.

If you are unsure of a certain issue and need to make a decision it might be a good day to wear some indigo. Indigo helps you find new creative ways to view a problem.

Indigo deepens mood and is a symbol of wisdom, self-mastery and spiritual realization. Indigo increases intuition. Indigo helps you connect with inner self; focus on resolving personal issues.

VIOLET MAGIC

You can have anything you want, if you want it badly enough. You can be anything you want to be, do anything you set out to accomplish if you hold to that desire with singleness of purpose. – Abraham Lincoln

Violet is the color of the seventh power center located in the crown of our heads. Put on some purple when you want to feel connected to a higher vibration.

Adding a little purple is a good way to make a guest feel very welcome. Violet is the color of royalty. Just a bit of violet infuses a room with a sense of wellness and being cared for.

Violet is a high vibrational color. When you need that extra boost or are just feeling down, it might be a good day for wearing violet.

PERSONAL INVITATION FROM MICHELE (AND SECRET PASS)

Whatever the mind can conceive and believe, it can achieve.
– Napoleon Hill

Hello Excellent Thriver!

Life, with its tenacious spirit will surprise you. Not every surprise is a pleasant or easy one, as we all know and can take on the skin of a tragedy, loss or challenge. Understandably, most people feel lost, broken or to blame during these difficult times.

Experience has also taught me, that with every challenge there is a hidden gem, a portal of strength that births us into the next brilliant version of ourselves. All you need are the right tools to find your brilliance. The very tools I discovered during my own journey, which taught me how to face forward, survive and ultimately thrive.

Facing forward for me meant becoming an expert at innovating out of the biggest curve ball life had ever thrown my way. My perfect life, the one I worked hard to build, the one that included a family I love, lay shattered when I found out I was diagnosed with aggressive facial cancer which ultimately left me disfigured.

My life became a roller coaster of surgery, dangerous infections and intense radiation. This extreme period in my life was filled with raw emotion and crushing realities. I had a smile that stopped traffic and gave people a reason to smile back. Ironically that was the very thing I would lose. I decided to sacrificed my right facial nerves for a chance to live.

My new paralyzed face ripped at the mask I hid behind for years and thrust me into a world of spirit, healing and intent. This was the beginning of my journey, a new beginning that guided me to turn inward and discover a deeper, stronger more brilliant self than I have ever known.

As a MBA who is curious and analytical by nature, I studied for over 10,000 hours everything from breathe work, how to align energy centers using scent and color, Qigong, Meditation, mindfulness, Ho'oponopno, Quantum Physics, poetry, affirmations, music and inspirational quotes, along the way I became a certified life coach. I dived deep into the nourishment of these resources to emerge with the awareness that like the tiny acorn, we all came programmed with everything we need to become a strong oak, to survive and thrive. We are the source of all things.

This center point of awareness came from what I call the Thrive Drive™. The Thrive Drive™ is the power center from where your innate ability to thrive and grow lives. When you align with Your Own Uniqueness (Y.O.U.) and engage the Thrive Drive, you become powerful signal drawing to you what you are being the cause of. It is the secret of this technique that entrains your feeling set point higher and higher...so you feel better and better and more good returns to your life.

I know you have been drawn to my story for a reason. Life has brought you a surprise of your own, but it has also brought you here, knowing you will have everything you need to shine. Let me give you the exact tools that helped me discover my Thrive Drive™ and support you in thriving out of any one of life's challenges.

As an award winning author, I have already helped tens of 1000s of people find the strength to overcome even the most shattering events. But I am not stopping there...

I have created an online portal to support you in an even deeper way. It's time to move past your fears, let go of negative thinking, take control and have the life you always wanted!

The journey is just beginning. Let's start together with this special free offer I created just for you: http://faceforwardyou.com/thrive-guide-gifts

Face Forward: Meeting Challenges Head On in Times of Trouble (Morgan James Publishing 2012)

Face Forward: Meeting Challenges Head On in Times of Trouble (Morgan James Publishing 2012)

Editorial Reviews

Michele's book shares (what) she has learned about as a wounded soldier who has lived…and learned from her experience about survival behavior. It is far better to read what she has learned about surviving and thriving than to have to learn from a personal disaster. ~ Bernie Siegel, MD author of Faith, Hope & Healing and A Book of Miracles

"These pages are inviting you to stop and realize what really matters. To stop and see how good you actually have it. To stop and consider what you really want to do with your life. ~ Kristen Moeller, MS Bestselling author, *Waiting for Jack: Confessions of a Self-Help Junkie – How to Stop Waiting and Start Living Your Life*

"We are not our circumstances. We are our possibilities.

Michele blows the doors off of cancer and show a big, bold, beautiful way of being face forward. No matter what you are facing in life..... face it with this book!"~ Suzanne Evans, Founder of Suzanne Evans Coaching LLC

Awaken your enthusiasm for life again! It is so easy to be paralyzed by fear. Michele's inspirational story proves most anything can be overcome. ~ *Eileen A Ginty, New York*

www.ingramcontent.com/pod-product-compliance
Lightning Source LLC
Chambersburg PA
CBHW070447050426
42451CB00015B/3378